Ten Poems
about Art

D1392882

ex libris

Candlestick Press

PUSHKIN
PRESS

Published by:
Candlestick Press,
Diversity House, 72 Nottingham Road, Arnold, Nottingham NG5 6LF
www.candlestickpress.co.uk

Design and typesetting by Craig Twigg

Printed by Ratcliff & Roper Print Group, Nottinghamshire, UK

Selection and Introduction © Geoff Dyer, 2019
www.geoffdyer.com

Cover illustration © Kvocek/Shutterstock

Candlestick Press monogram © Barbara Shaw, 2008

© Candlestick Press, 2019

Donation to Teapot Trust
https://www.teapot-trust.org/

ISBN 978 1 907598 77 7

Acknowledgements:

The poems in this pamphlet are reprinted from the following books, all by
permission of the publishers listed unless stated otherwise. Every effort has been
made to trace the copyright holders of the poems published in this book. The
editor and publisher apologise if any material has been included without
permission or without the appropriate acknowledgement, and would be glad to be
told of anyone who has not been consulted.

Thanks are due to all the copyright holders cited below for their kind permission:
Moniza Alvi, *Split Word: Poems 1990 - 2005* (Bloodaxe Books, 2005)
www.bloodaxebooks.com. Fleur Adcock, *Poems 1960 - 2000* (Bloodaxe
Books, 2000) www.bloodaxebooks.com. WH Auden, *Collected Poems*
(Random House Inc., 1975; Faber & Faber, 1994), Copyright © 1975, 1994
by WH Auden, by permission of Curtis Brown Ltd. Mark Doty, *Atlantic*
(HarperCollins, 1996; Random House UK, 1997). Linda France, *Red* (Bloodaxe
Books, 1997) by kind permission of the author. Sue Hubbard, *Ghost Station*
(Salt, 2004). Mimi Khalvati, *Selected Poems* (Carcanet Press, 2000).
RS Thomas, *Between Here and Now* (Orion Books, 1981). Tomas Tranströmer,
The Half-Finished Heaven: Selected Poems, trans. Robert Bly (Graywolf
Press, 2017). William Carlos Williams, *Collection Poems 1939 - 1962* (New
Directions Publishing Corp. © 1962).

All permissions cleared courtesy of Swift Permissions
(swiftpermissions@gmail.com).

Where poets are no longer living, their dates are given.

Introduction

Joseph Brodsky, contemplating a photograph of WH Auden, "began to wonder whether one form of art was capable of depicting another, whether the visual could apprehend the semantic." And how about the other way around, the semantic apprehending the visual?

The answer, from all manner of poets and artists, has been a resounding yes. Baudelaire, for example, in his *Salon of 1846*, writes that "the best account of a picture may well be a sonnet or an elegy".

I've been drawn to poems about works of art for almost as long as I've been interested in paintings. I like the sense of encounter and dialogue, the romance or randomness of a first meeting giving way to reflection and meditation. But the power of that first moment or first glimpse is invariably preserved in and by the subsequent contemplation in a way that the rigorous demands of art history can sometimes dull or even forget. It's a reminder that art, while often seen in a museum, is part of our lived experience, as much a part of being alive as falling in love.

So, over the years, whenever I've come across a poem about a work of art, I've kept a note or copy in a folder in the hope of one day putting together an anthology of such works. As this folder grew so the dialogues extended. William Carlos Williams, for example, is addressing not just a painting (Brueghel's *Icarus*) but is tacitly engaged in a conversation with WH Auden's earlier account of that painting.

Naturally I thought this was a highly original project but then I discovered that there's actually a word for poems addressing works of art, and that writing so-called ekphrastic poems constitutes a fairly standard exercise in poetry-writing courses. Well, I suppose there's a word for everything, and although, ideally, this word would not have taken up residence in my brain, my affection for – and my desire to discover new – poems about works of art remains undiminished.

Geoff Dyer

Musée des Beaux Arts

About suffering they were never wrong,
The Old Masters: how well they understood
Its human position; how it takes place
While someone else is eating or opening a window or just walking
                                                    dully along;
How, when the aged are reverently, passionately waiting
For the miraculous birth, there always must be
Children who did not specially want it to happen, skating
On a pond at the edge of the wood:
They never forgot
That even the dreadful martyrdom must run its course
Anyhow in a corner, some untidy spot
Where the dogs go on with their doggy life and the torturer's horse
Scratches its innocent behind on a tree.

In Brueghel's *Icarus*, for instance: how everything turns away
Quite leisurely from the disaster; the ploughman may
Have heard the splash, the forsaken cry,
But for him it was not an important failure; the sun shone
As it had to on the white legs disappearing into the green
Water; and the expensive delicate ship that must have seen
Something amazing, a boy falling out of the sky,
Had somewhere to get to and sailed calmly on.

WH Auden (1907 – 1973)

Nude in Bathtub
after Bonnard

Between the edge of the afternoon
and dusk, between the bath's white
rim and the band of apricot light,
she bathed, each day, as if dreaming.

From the doorway he noted
her right foot hooked for balance
beneath the enamel lip, body
and water all one in a miasma

of mist, a haze of lavender blue.
Such intimacy. A woman, two walls,
a chequered floor, the small
curled dog basking in a pool

of sun reflected from the tiles
above the bath. Outside
the throbbing heat. So many times
he has drawn her, caught the obsessive

soaping of her small breasts,
compressed the crouched frame into
his picture space, the nervy movements
that hemmed in his life.

The house exudes her still,
breathes her from each sunlit corner,
secretes her lingering smell
from shelves of rosewood *armoires*,

and the folded silk *chemises*
he doesn't have the heart to touch.
And from the landing, his memory tricks,
as through the open door the smudged

floor glistens with silvered tracks,
her watered foot prints to and from
the tub where she floats in almond oil
deep in her sarcophagus of light.

Sue Hubbard

Four Cut Sunflowers, One Upside Down

Turbulent stasis on a blue ground.

What is any art but static flame?
Fire of spun gold, grain.

This brilliant flickering's

arrested by named (Naples,
chrome, cadmium) and nameless

yellows, tawny golds. Look

at the ochre sprawl – *how*
they sprawl, these odalisques,

withering coronas
around the seedheads' intricate precision.

Even drying, the petals curling
into licks of fire,

they're haloed in the pure rush of light
yellow is. One theory of colour,

before Newton broke the world
through the prism's planes

and nailed the primaries to the wheel,
posited that everything's made of yellow

and blue – coastal colours
which engender, in their coupling,

every other hue, so that the world's
an elaborate dialogue

between citron and Prussian blue.
They are a whole summer to themselves.

They are a nocturne
in argent and gold, and they burn

with the ferocity
of dying (which is to say, the luminosity

of what's living *hardest*). Is it a human soul
the painter's poured

into them – thin, beleaguered old word,
but what else to call it?

Evening is overtaking them.
In this last light they are voracious.

Mark Doty

Edward Hopper's *Hotel Room* (1931)

What the hell am I doing here,
a cheap hotel room in Baltimore?

The crowded streetcar reeked of greasy
done-in flesh. I looked so classy

in my new cloche and heels, it ruined
the effect. They pinch my feet. It's good

to get them off. I've read this letter
too many times already. The elevator

was out of order. I walked up three flights,
counting each stair. Room twenty-five.

It's passably clean but cramped,
with a monstrous chair, old-fashioned, emerald,

and leftover layers of other people's affairs.
What did I expect? Straight after work, he says,

he'll call by. A whole night and breakfast
together before he drives on up to the Adirondacks

to join his wife and kids. He's signed it just
with his initial, a thin spidery kiss.

I told Mom and Dad their little girl's
staying over at Doreen and Earl's

place; they're covering for me. I wanted
this. When we're apart I feel so odd,

incomplete. But that's how it is right now. Maybe
someday he'll leave his kids, and her, for me.

I saw this movie at the Ritz the other day...
Aw, sitting here, I'm getting nervous, the way

I am waiting to see my dentist. We've never
gone all the way before. All that yellow,

like eggs, sunny-side up, turns my stomach,
the puce counterpane. Hope he'll crack

some bourbon. It's ten after six. Guess
I ought to dress. Just so he can take it off again.   .

Jesus, I'm scared. What am I doing here?
It wasn't like this in the movie.

Linda France

Cézanne

The Card Players

And neither of them has said:
 Your lead.
  An absence of trumps
will arrest movement.

  Knees almost touching,
  hands almost touching,
   they are far away
in time in a world
  of equations.

  The pipe without
 smoke, the empty
 bottle, the light
on the wall are the clock
  they go by.
   Only their minds
   lazily as flies
    drift
round and round the inane
problem their boredom
  has led them to pose.

RS Thomas (1913 – 2000)

I Would Like to be a Dot in a Painting by Miró

I would like to be a dot in a painting by Miró.

Barely distinguishable from other dots,
it's true, but quite uniquely placed.
And from my dark centre

I'd survey the beauty of the linescape
and wonder – would it be worthwhile
to roll myself towards the lemon stripe,

Centrally poised, and push my curves
against its edge, to get myself
a little extra attention?

But it's fine where I am.
I'll never make out what's going on
around me, and that's the joy of it.

The fact that I'm not a perfect circle
makes me more interesting in this world.
People will stare forever –

Even the most unemotional get excited.
So here I am, on the edge of animation,
a dream, a dance, a fantastic construction,

A child's adventure.
And nothing in this tawny sky
can get too close, or move too far away.

Moniza Alvi

From *Interiors*

after Edouard Vuillard

Edouard Vuillard (1868 – 1940) lived with his mother until her death when he was 50. Mme. Vuillard was a seamstress and her workroom, like his studio, was part of the home. 'The home and the studio were one, and the honour of the home and the honour of the studio the same honour. What resulted? Everything was a rhythm, a rite and a ceremony from the moment of rising. Everything was a sacred event...'

(Charles Péguy, l'Argent)

The Parlour

Between cup and lip,
needle and cloth,
the closing of a cupboard door
and reassertion of a room,

in those pauses when the head lifts
and time stands still

what gesture slips its epoch
to evoke another continent?
What household conjures household

in the homogeneity of furniture,
rituals that find their choirs
in morning light, evening lamps,
cloths and clothes and screens?

This woman sewing,
man reading at his desk,
in raising eyes towards the wall
do they lose themselves in foliage,

sense themselves receding
to become presences on gravel paths
and in becoming incorporeal
free to be transposed?

Do they see themselves and not themselves
– have any sense how manifold
might be their incarnations –
in the needlepoint of walls and skies
so distant from their own?

For this profile hazed
against shutterfold and sky
has as many claimants
as there are flowers on the wall,
in a vase, on a dress, in the air

and everywhere, like leaves,
recognitions drop their calling-cards
on a mood, a table set for supper,

disperse themselves as freely
as the mille-fleurs from a palette,

settle unobtrusively
as her to her sewing, him to his book,
lowering eyes from vistas
that have brought them to themselves.

Mimi Khalvati

Vermeer

It's not a sheltered world. The noise begins over there, on the
    other side of the wall
where the alehouse is
with its laughter and quarrels, its rows of teeth, its tears, its
    chiming of clocks,
and the psychotic brother-in-law, the murderer, in whose
    presence everyone feels fear.

The huge explosion and the emergency crew arriving late,
boats showing off on the canals, money slipping down into
    pockets – the wrong man's –
ultimatum piled on ultimatum,
wide-mouthed red flowers whose sweat reminds us of
    approaching war.

And then straight through the wall – from there – straight into
    the airy studio
and the seconds that have got permission to live for centuries.
Paintings that choose the name: *The Music Lesson*
or *A Woman in Blue Reading a Letter.*
She is eight months pregnant, two hearts beating inside her.
The wall behind her holds a crinkly map of Terra Incognita.

Just breathe. An unidentifiable blue fabric has been tacked to
    the chairs.
Gold-headed tacks flew in with astronomical speed
and stopped smack there
as if they had always been stillness and nothing else.

The ears experience a buzz, perhaps it's depth or perhaps height.
It's the pressure from the other side of the wall,
the pressure that makes each fact float
and makes the brushstroke firm.

Passing through walls hurts human beings, they get sick from it,
but we have no choice.
It's all one world. Now to the walls.
The walls are a part of you.
One either knows that, or one doesn't; but it's the same for
    everyone
except for small children. There aren't any walls for them.

The airy sky has taken its place leaning against the wall.
It is like a prayer to what is empty.
And what is empty turns its face to us
and whispers:
"I am not empty, I am open."

Tomas Tranströmer (1931 – 2015)
Translated by Robert Bly

Leaving the Tate

Coming out with your clutch of postcards
in a Tate Gallery bag and another clutch
of images packed into your head you pause
on the steps to look across the river

and there's a new one: light bright buildings,
a streak of brown water, and such a sky
you wonder who painted it – Constable? No:
too brilliant. Crome? No: too ecstatic –

a madly pure Pre-Raphaelite sky,
perhaps, sheer blue apart from the white plumes
rushing up it (today, that is,
April. Another day would be different

but it wouldn't matter. All skies work.)
Cut to the lower right for a detail:
seagulls pecking on mud, below
two office blocks and a Georgian terrace.

Now swing to the left, and take in plane trees
bobbled with seeds, and that brick building,
and a red bus... Cut it off just there,
by the lamp-post. Leave the scaffolding in.

That's your next one. Curious how
these outdoor pictures didn't exist
before you'd looked at the indoor pictures,
the ones on the walls. But here they are now,

marching out of their panorama
and queuing up for the viewfinder
your eye's become. You can isolate them
by holding your optic muscles still.

You can zoom in on figure studies
(that boy with the rucksack), or still lives,
abstracts, townscapes. No one made them.
The light painted them. You're in charge

of the hanging committee. Put what space
you like around the ones you fix on,
and gloat. Art multiplies itself.
Art's whatever you choose to frame.

Fleur Adcock

Landscape with the Fall of Icarus

According to Brueghel
when Icarus fell
it was spring

a farmer was ploughing
his field
the whole pageantry

of the year was
awake tingling
near

the edge of the sea
concerned
with itself

sweating in the sun
that melted
the wings' wax

unsignificantly
off the coast
there was

a splash quite unnoticed
this was
Icarus drowning

William Carlos Williams (1883 – 1963)